Poems
of
the
River
Spirit

PITT POETRY SERIES

Ed Ochester, Editor

Poems
of
the
River
Spirit

Maurice
Kilwein
Guevara

University of
Pittsburgh Press

Published by the University of Pittsburgh Press, Pittsburgh, Pa. 15260
Copyright © 1996, Maurice Kilwein Guevara
All rights reserved
Manufactured in the United States of America
Printed on acid-free paper

Library of Congress Cataloging-in-Publication data and acknowledgments
are located at the end of this book.

A CIP catalog record for this book is available from the British Library.
Eurospan, London

The publication of this book is supported by grants
from the National Endowment for the Arts
in Washington, D.C., a Federal agency,
and the Pennsylvania Council on the Arts.

In memory of my friends
now in the Seventh Circle, Second Ring

La embocadura del río empezó
con un bostezo que duró mil años.

— Janet Jennerjohn

Contents

The Other World

The River Spirits

I

Feliz noche bajo las estrellas rojas.
— Gonzalo Arango

Think of me as a rat
the size of a pistol,
my tail tight like a twisted bill,
the quick slip of me into shadows.

Think of me as a river spirit,
studying the broken green glass and the rusted spike,
imitating the way the dead immigrants spoke,
watching the barges like black corpses
drift in the reflected mill fire,
waiting, always waiting for the ghost train,
the one that comes at 2:05 and full of freight.

Think of me as the rat
unseen in the weeds until the clouds move,
my wings wet like oil in the moonlight,
and the stars, the stars of Pittsburgh in my tiny eyes.

II

In the blue and sleeping hours
I waited at the point where the Allegheny
and Monongahela bleed into one
In the hours of sirens and chemical trains
I stared up at the stars and brown bats
at the pricks of yellow light in the foothills
at the reflected moon breaking up into river waves
and waited a bridge away
from jobless men gathered near a burning drum
from the girl I could not see
in the back seat of the junked Nova
I waited while nothing like spirits
dragged themselves up
one by one
onto the concrete wharf
I saw only a mother rat
gnawing pale newsprint by a garbage can
as the wind
occasionally
lifted a page
like the flea-dotted wing of a vulture

III

By few accounts it was a jewelled lake that spring,
       but for the lovely families of Pittsburgh
who could get away to fish, to hunt, to lounge, to love,
       under parasol, the latest novel from New York,
for the Mellons and Fricks and Carnegies,
       the dammed resort stocked with black bass
was paradise, and the price nothing short of a steal:
       what did the state of Pennsylvania care?
Hands were washed, lunch of pheasant prepared,
       crystals filled high with Montrachet.
Two men spoke of the Union Trust Company.
       Another said nothing of the dam, nothing of repairs.
Before adieux, the wives agreed; all loved this haven,
       while a final voice praised the purity of the air.

The rain started the day before and fell on the American flags,
       on the horses and their riders, on the brass instruments,
on the immigrants and the natives. The parade to honor the dead
       of Johnstown ended early. All that long night
the mountain streams filled, rushing down the valley.
       Lake Conemaugh was rising. By late morning,
the dam was brimming: more and more water. What was her name
       who received the tapped-out warning? Then the second.
At 2:45 P.M., the third and last before she died, the wire humming:
       "The dam is becoming dangerous and may possibly go."
It collapsed, pushed everything forward. Into history.
       Locomotives swam for miles. Who understood the church bells,
the mill whistles? Iron bridges danced and houses flew. After the great fires,
       the missing were found as far away as Pittsburgh and Cincinnati.

IV

Once when the Italian girl
pumped the handle
to open the faucet
at Ellis Island
no water came
only the brown shiny head
of a water bug

V

So much snow falling suddenly
over the crisscrossed tracks
of the B&O train yard
that the capped man shoveling coal
into the rusty wheelbarrow
thinks back to moths
fifty years earlier
in Wales

That breezy summer he was eight
and already helping at the colliery
usher two tan ponies
one by one
into the stony mouth
into the huddled coughing pit
and out again
brushing feeding watering

He was lacing his boots outside
in the dark dumb dawn
when the men from first shift
approached
clean-faced and quiet
Old Davey Jones said
No need to go to the stable
We already give the ponies some apples
Colliery Three is shut down for a while

Alone on the porch stoop the boy sat
mutely aware
as three white moths flew in the morning chill
and a fourth landed on his boot
that by noon the carpenter would need extra help

From the bridge I saw a tiny figure in the snow
push a wheelbarrow toward the gray shanty

VI

That dude named Homer Brown
played for the Homestead Grays
second base
hands quick like a piano man
gold eyetooth
thin waist
little hair right here
under his lip
Didn't never talk much
even before he went to the war

The war
the big fucking ugly war no one remembers now
you know
I know cause I served in the Pacific Theater
Homer was in France
artillery I believe
That's where he learned to be a mechanic
Yes sir a mechanic
over there in France
before one stupid German shell
blew off his left arm

Thing about Homer Brown
when he got home
he didn't take a goddamn benefit from the army
He refused it all
G.I. Bill
V.A. hospital
no insurance
nothing
not a goddamn thing

Homer went back to live with his mother
in that same row house on Second Avenue
he grew up in
Got a job at Massey Buick
in transmissions
You
know
how
many
tiny
little
parts
automatic
transmissions got
Homer learned to take them apart
put them back together again
with his chin his shoulder and his quick right hand

VII

Crude
said the educated son of the Polish ironworker
by the tiled coop in the little backyard

You still eat lard on day-old bread
You smell like pipe smoke and sweat
You still have a bucket on every floor
and dump your piss in the toilet
For Christ's sake Pap
I don't understand
Now you're retired
you could have carpet in the front room
new curtains
a real headstone for Mum
get your teeth fixed
get Sears to put in storm doors
right from the factory
Let's face it
Tata
everything you make is crude

The old man in undershirt and black suspenders
spit a clot of Cutty Pipe into the cindered dirt
unlatched the coop for a second
reached in with one hand
and pulled out a pigeon the dirty color of the sky

Bullshit
the father said
walking toward the kitchen
Least what I make works

VIII

Brick and metal. Dirty brick and old raw iron.
— Jack Gilbert

Yes the bus will take you to Hazelwood
a steel town where my grandparents coughed
laughed and sucked in the black particulate air
there on the last street then charcoal shanties
the B&O the Mon River   I was saying to someone
the sun would be shining on the tomato plants and the peppers
in the little backyards of the immigrants and the natives
Grandpa Hans old railroader
a golden mug of beer in his crotch
rolls a Top with Cutty Pipe the orange glow at his mouth
a burning shred falling on his undershirt
Vhat you say Mudder
maybe me you go upshtairs for some luf
and my Italian *abuelita* would be a little angry
and a little happy on the porch swing in the orange twilight
Hans you're going to set yourself on fire
Oh Hans the way you talk
Look at that shirt   È fatta la frittata

From the kitchen there is stardust
My father puts the alto together
adjusts the mouthpiece mouths the reed with spit
tells my mother *What it really needs* mouths
What it really needs is a whole new set of pads
He blows my father blows stardust from the golden brass
his eyes closed   This world hangs from his neck like a burden
What is my mother looking at what pattern of crumbs
cinders on the oilcloth

Don't fall my grandmother warns as I circle
the thin ledge surrounding the porch
My uncle Bernie is coming home from Vietnam
his duffels full of army surplus   Drugs
fatigues guns fill the dining room of his return
There will be no body bag by the steps
He hugs me and my brothers like life
And this will happen when he buys the red Mustang
He'll be hungry for women
Most nights he'll drink till he's drunk as a corpse
He'll join the N.R.A. sleepwalk lift weights work on his car
Stone sober one day he'll shoot his rifle
fire it straight into the coke-rotten skies over Pittsburgh
then go into the kitchen and make himself a sandwich

This way   From downtown catch the 56C to Hazelwood
It's only ten minutes and you're halfway there
when everything starts to stink of mills   When I was a boy
I used to sleep with my brothers on the floor of Grandpa's bedroom
We'd all use the same iron bucket to piss in
I do remember laughter
and then the quiet
watching through the window the fire blossom from the stack
of the Jones and Laughlin blast furnace   And listening
trains coupling in the night thunder a windup clock ticking in the dark

IX

A lightning storm
Mount Washington at night
looking down over the city
dark wind
rain waiting like a panther
then the spasm of everything bright

X

She denied it to everyone
to her mother
to her father
to the nun who called her a slut in gym class
to the boy who said See it felt good didn't it
to the kind sister visiting from the Philippines
to Jesus who took away the drops of blood
to herself and the wet pillow
to the little feet kicking
even to the lightning bugs
and finally to no one at all
that evening her mother was at bingo
and her father was working second shift setup

She rose
the black & white TV on
Lucy hiding under a table
as Desi swore in Spanish and the horizontal started to go
There was a piece of watermelon in the sink
She took the paring knife
left the back door open
and walked slowly down to the river

Precinct 5 got a call just after midnight
something about a Chevy on blocks
and a baby crying by the Mon
and God
she was sorry
she couldn't give her name

XI

Warm winter
spring green and generous
Mrs. Zomock
no teeth and from the Old Country
wears her white hair in a black net
Agitated in her brown house dress
she is tall bent pretty as a broom
at work on her back steps
sweeping sweeping
dem gahtdamn cahterpeelers avay

There's just the one tree in her tiny backyard
She drinks hot black coffee at the kitchen table
and stares out the window day after day
One eye sees only a milky cocoon of everything
It's with the good eye
in her native Hungarian
she counts up the silky tents of caterpillars
in the branching necks and elbows of the tree
Fuzzy worms moving
fingers in a womb
is what she tells me by the wire fence

After Mass Sunday morning
all the children dressed in bright colors
spread out like flowers
on the steps of St. Stephen's
Mrs. Zomock's happy
as she crosses the avenue
crosses the bridge over the railroad tracks
where her dead husband worked thirty-eight years
sees the fire stack from the mill and coughs
In her dark basement
she puts a live match to sheet rags
she has bundled on the end of a stubbed broom
and soaked with lighter fluid
There's even a fiery glow in the bad eye
as she climbs the old stairs with her torch

The first cocoon in the tree blossoms in a single flame
the second and third as well
Several leaves hiss like beetles
just before the orange clump of rags falls suddenly
into her hairnet and face

Zomock Neni lived almost five more years
with her daughter-in-law and son in the suburbs
difficult in simple ways and completely blind

XII

Last or next or first
I stood on the crown of Pittsburgh Plate Glass
or
seventy stories down the pit of a mine
and opened in my hands the invisible book
from which I sang
Death came to the tiny green frog
Death gutted out the black belly of my hills
Death prayed with the old widows
Death saw a million arrows and liquid steel
Death hissed like a beetle startled by a workboot
Spoke broken Croatian English Death
Death came with the Light Man
Death came with the Gas Man
Death yanked the huckster's bell
Death took tickets at the Whip and let the little ones sneak by
Death was the cat picking at the fish with two heads
Mrs. Death and her daughter worked overtime during the war
Death snowed on bridges and roofs and playgrounds
Death called out Bingo Bingo Bingo here
Frick with Mellon and Death firing up Cuban cigars
Death smelled corn bread frying on the Hill
Death wore hunters' orange or Communion white
Death was a Bohunk
Death was a Polack
Death was a Nigger
Death was a Dago
Death was a shot and an Iron City and yes
Death even wore eyeglasses
and sometimes a white shirt
or carried a black bag
and left through the green cellar doors at dawn

XIII

TUKAJ POCIVA
FRANK KOVAC
ROJEN 1891
UMRL 22 JAN. 1923
LAHKA TI BUDI
AMERISKA
ZEMLAJA NEPOZABLJENI
SI OD
KOVAC

I'm not sure of some of the letters

FRANCIS A. FAITH
PENNSYLVANIA
TEC 5 291 ENGR COMBAT B N
MARCH 3, 1923   JUNE 2, 1954

STEVE CHUPA
DIED
MARCH 23, 1915
AGED 25
KILLED IN STEEL MILL

A tent worm is crawling down the gray stone

UMW
OF
AMERICA
DEDICATED
TO THE MEMORY OF
NICOLA MACERA
FOR DISTINGUISHED SERVICE AND SELF-SACRIFICE
IN THE CAUSE OF LABOR AND ADVANCEMENT
OF THE UNITED MINE WORKERS OF AMERICA

an iron cross
welded in a cellar
pushed into a hole
filled crudely
with cement
has rusted
and fallen
and lies in the June grass

KANAGUNDA
SZYBIST
DIED 1923
MOTHER

OVDE UPOCCIVAUMIRU
JOSIP KRESCO
RODIESE
MAR. 20, 1893
PODHUMU HERCEGOVINA
UMRO OCTOBER 27, 1921

and this only one hill
of a Catholic cemetery

IT NYUGSZIK
SZABO LAJOS
SZULETET 1899 JULY 27
MEGHALT 1922 FEB. 16
NYUGODJON BEKEVEL

SALVATORE FRONTERA
1888–1920

QUI RIPOSA
ANGELINA
BRANDINI
NATA 1876
MORTA 1924
LASCIA 3 FIGLIE

the little ones
forever
on the outskirts
of the cemetery

VELIA FORESI
1925–1926

SUSIE KLEIN
BORN AUG. 10 1920
DIED JAN. 19 1921

FRANZ XAVERI.
SON OF
F. & C. SCHILLING
BORN JAN. 23, 1866
DIED DEC. 3, 1869

HERMAN ANTON
SON OF
F. & C. SCHILLING
BORN MAR 31 1868
DIED DEC 10 1869

Zapata Olivella told us
to understand a people
first see how they bury the dead
then go to their market

JOE SENOK
KILLED JUNE 12
1918
AT GRACETON 6
FLAT BY CHAIN
MACHINE

MADRE
ROSARIA CULLUCCI
MARITATA TULLIO
APR. 3 1879
MAR. 12 1912
EARNEST

my arm is turning pink and red
in the sun

RIPOSA LANIMA DI
CATARINA PERRI
NATA L'ANNO 1882
MORTA IL 26 MARZO
1914 LASCIANDO LO
SPOSO CON I FIGLI
IN GRAN DOLORE

this one has her picture
sepia
three drops under the cracked
oval glass
it must have been her wedding day

ALAS VALENTOVIC
DIED JUNE 19, 1913
AGED 23 YRS

IRENE O'HARA SHELTON
1895–1969

JOZEF CRNODYA
LETA ROJEN 1918
MARCA RADIV 8
UNERU FAEBRUJAR
6, 1919   VECNA LUC
MAJITI LVETI

who still puts flowers

HENRY P. HORN
DIED JULY 5 1918
AGED 80 YEARS
3 DAYS

my son's two-year voice
calling
from the street where he sees me
my wife telling him in Spanish
not to run

XIV

. . . the rat population is probably equal to the human population.
—*New Columbia Encyclopedia*

One rat under the snow sleeps invisible.
One rat eats blueberries in the dark.
That one is climbing aboard the galleon of history.
Each of us has a twin desire
to hibernate in another body.

Tonight I am swimming the Ohio, wanting to fly.
Sister, dreamer, hoarder,
cornered fighter to the death,
pillager of the small blue eggs of birds,
epicure of chicken, duck, turkey, sweet pigeon,
lover of Indian corn, of hemp and paintbrush,
landscape artist, tunnel maker,
mate, destroyer of whole libraries,
nightmare in the sweet dreams of the candle maker,
brother, stargazer, ordinary creature,
how could I not love you
　　　　　as I love myself in the moonbright water?

Suddenly, these black wings,
the rudiments of *paraíso:*
I rise and lift, lift myself up
out of the Ohio.

The Neck of the Air

A Rhyme for Halloween

Tonight I light the candles of my eyes in the lee
And swing down this branch full of red leaves.
Yellow moon, skull and spine of the hare,
Arrow me to town on the neck of the air.

I hear the undertaker make love in the heather;
The candy maker, poor fellow, is under the weather.
Skunk, moose, raccoon, they go to the doors in threes
With a torch in their hands or pleas: "O, please . . . "

Baruch Spinoza and the butcher are drunk:
One is the tail and one is the trunk
Of a beast who dances in circles for beer
And doesn't think twice to learn how to steer.

Our clock is blind, our clock is dumb.
Its hands are broken, its fingers numb.
No time for the martyr of our fair town
Who wasn't a witch because she could drown.

Now the dogs of the cemetery are starting to bark
At the vision of her, bobbing up through the dark.
When she opens her mouth to gasp for air,
A moth flies out and lands in her hair.

The apples are thumping, winter is coming.
The lips of the pumpkin soon will be humming.
By the caw of the crow on the first of the year,
Something will die, something appear.

Long Distance

(two Sundays before Lucilita's coma)

Pennsylvania to the coast of Ecuador, my mother calling her aunt,
the nurse picking up, relaying the phone, and the woman
under the sheet says nothing. This morning I saw Walt Whitman
half-buried in the blowing snow of the foothills. This was two weeks ago:
my mother saying in Spanish to the silent woman *We miss you*
We love you   We think of you every day   and waiting
the four thousand miles. Delay. *Lucilita.* Saying nothing.
Until finally, my mother asks ¿*Me oyes?* Do you hear me?
Te oigo: the only words the old woman says. I hear you.
Singing under the snow. Singing under the falling snow.

A Little Thing

I think I saw a rat in the kitchen.
It may have been a mouse.
It may have been a dried leaf or crumpled page
scurrying behind the electric stove.
The window was open.
It could have been nothing more than a little pink tail of sunlight
vanishing under the sink.

When the Light Turned Red

In the Strip District I saw a steel-colored fish
lying in a box of white ice
I saw the refrigerated truck
filled with Colombian roses
unload at the flower market
I smelled chicken smoke
rise from the black Cambodian grill
I saw two teenagers in filthy T-shirts
sitting exhausted on crates and passing a joint
I saw Luigi from Parma
who turns seventy this year
kiss my wife three times
in the Italian way
A gray cat sprayed a dumpster in the alley
I saw a cop eating from a styrofoam cup
I heard a Vietnamese grandmother
sweeping water into the street
As I threw my sandwich paper
into a wire basket and to the busy flies
the sun came out
and shone on a pile of lemons in a cart
on an open crate of striped watermelons
on blueberries in the green paper baskets
on the tomatoes and peppers and yellow zucchini
We went to the coffee market
and bought one pound of beans from Guatemala
one pound from Ethiopia
one pound from Cundinamarca
We went to the Mexican store para tortillas
from Chicago y queso añejo y chorizo
We listened
as two black women laughed and laughed in the bread store
A suburban man told his toddler not to touch anything
A large truck backed up
Something stunk
A jet flew overhead
The meat cutter finally came out of the meat shop
his apron white with brown smears

and smoked a cigarette by the newspaper box
A famous person had been murdered in Cleveland
The bells of St. Stan's started ringing
It was four o'clock in the afternoon
A woman with a babushka bumped into me
Three pigeons landed on a gutter
When the light turned red
the Iron City truck squealed to a stop
then the mattress truck
Then it was quiet enough for a second
for me to hear my favorite word in English
downtown

U-turn

Mrs. Vicky Maggio from Bloomfield
learned in Italy how to cry when necessary
at the funeral of a nosey neighbor
or for this cop with the shiny black boots
who asks why she did a U-turn
on such a busy street and is she nuts
Instead of *coupons* or *bingo chips*
Truth is she snivels *I forgot to turn*
my husband over
so he don't get bedsores
on top of his slipped disk and
Sure honey I got a driver's license and
Thank you
See you a good boy
Be careful now
Here it's windy
and she gives him a wild cherry cough drop
as she drives slowly away with the handbrake on

Doña Josefina Counsels Doña Concepción Before Entering Sears

Conchita debemos to speak totalmente in English
cuando we go into Sears okay   Por qué
Porque didn't you hear lo que pasó   It say
on the eleven o'clock news anoche que two robbers
was caught in Sears and now this is the part
I'm not completely segura que I got everything
porque channel 2 tiene tú sabes that big fat guy
that's hard to understand porque his nose sit on his lip
like a elefante pues the point es que the robbers the police say
was two young men pretty big y one have a hairy face
and the other is calvo that's right he's baldy and okay
believe me qué barbaridad porque Hairy Face
and Mister Baldy goes right into the underwear department
takes all the money from the caja yeah uh-huh the cash register
and mira Mister Baldy goes to this poor Italian woman that I
guess would be like us sixty o sixty-five who is in the section
of the back-support brassieres and he makes her put a big bra
over her head para que she can't see nothing and kneel
like she's talking to God to save her poor life
and other things horrible pero the point como dije
es que there was two of them and both was speaking Spanish
y por eso is a good thing Conchita so the people at Sears
don't confuse us with Hairy and Baldy that we speak English only
okay ready
            Oh what a nice day to be aquí en Sears Miss Conception

How Grammar School Is Changing

In the early years all of the teachers were Nouns. They were very strict Nouns. They wore black robes that reached to the floor and had a fondness for caning the palms of your hands. In the beginning there was very little light; then a window was placed in the east wall of the school. The first Verb to enter the classroom through our new and only window was a Be. It was yellow and black and buzzed by my ear. One day Be walked vertically up the world map from Santiago to Santa Marta and stopped to smell the salt water. Thinking twice, it flew up to Florida and was eyeing Orange County when my mean third grade Noun squashed Be with her big white reader. She said, "We only need one river in this town," which didn't make any sense. It wasn't long, however, before more stuff started coming in through the windows (there were soon four) and through the new fire doors and down the chimney: Adjectives with big, bright, yellow and orange, polka-dot bow ties; Adverbs who yodeled longingly for their homeland; a Pronoun who wore cornrows with green ribbons (I confess I had my first crush on She); a family of Silver Brackets; Question Marks and Periods snowed down the chimney; and, finally, the Invisible Etceteras — pranksters that they are — started moaning sweet nothings in my Noun's ear, which made her grin a little, thank God. By the time I was in the fifth grade, after a vicious fight with the village elders, the principal had hired Dr. Miguel de Sustantivo to make the school bilingual: *y tú sabes lo que pasó después: vinieron las familias Adjetivo y Pronombre y Verbo y más y más. . . .* But yesterday a new little someone came from far, far away who sits sad all alone at lunch. Does anyone know a few words in Vietnamese? I would like to say Good Morning.

Once When I Was in the Eighth Grade

I got caught staring out the window when the bells were ringing
Maybe you want to tell everybody what's so interesting
There's a man with a bottle of wine walking toward the mill
He's wearing rags and the rags are burning blue
In one of his palms there is a green bird
hatchling of the sewing box   She breathes once
every time the earth walks around the sun   I heard her sing
before they used her soft green body in the mines

After that he let me stare out the window the rest of the year

Dorothy, Dear

> Unusual weather we're havin', ain't it.
> — The Cowardly Lion

I must be in New York
because the toilet's running snow's falling
it's April 1st 1994
and by the time I reach the street
I'm out of breath watching the rich ladies
big as apartment buildings
walking poodles prairie dogs a praying mantis
and a Colombian Mambo Queen holds his thin arms out
balancing barefoot
doing his best La Quebrada atop a fireplug
I say Every snow's a white flood in this city
He says *Qué tú sabes del dolor que tengo yo*
I'm all them Wizard freaks in one: Scaredy Crow
León   Tin Boy   Talking Tree   Flying Waldorf Monkey
He keeps talking as I turn around and away by the Ocean
Liberty's still wearing that prom dress copper and rented
and holding a torch for some dead French guy
and the T-shaped Mambo behind me mumbling
Ain't no Mago   Just go home Girl   Wherever you from
Milwaukee Jupiter Pittsburgh   Take the train Girl
Ain't no way no Mago going to fly you out of this storm

A City Prophet Talks to God on the 56C to Hazelwood

I say
Seems like everyone's sleepy as the Chessie cat
I say Captain
look at your river old Monongahela
Even John the Baptist would not wade in that water
Never mind I know the catfish big as sharks
Hmm mm Hmm mm
And the things they pull up from there
the bones of horses the bodies of men
grand pianos pig iron toilets Singer sewing machines
two railroad ties crossed
spiked at the breastbone
old cars even parking meters down there time expired

God
don't be like the people tell their children sit far away
like the man from the State says Take your pill Take your pill
Don't talk back cause you might alarm the other passengers
But he says I know you know they know
they're just puppet voices in your head
You think my brain's polluted with intergalactic debris
I think we're all lice on a fat rat's back
rolling down the incline
into the river of the Anti-World
Smile
while the orphan child dresses us for the wake
Wake
and suffer the wildflowers to come unto me
Hazelwood Avenue
Ring the bell Ring the bell
I say
Even the Turk's-cap of God will rust in the Garden of Old Raw Iron
I say
This is my stop
This is where I step down

Beyond Kigali

Who will remember the girl in yellow robes
walking down the hillside in the rain,
balancing
the straw bushel of green coffee?

The Miniaturist

I make tiny, tiny huts,
the hills, too, are tiny,
small hills, small trees,
a silver river, a forge with smoke,
and a little blue water tower.

To work on such a minute scale,
I use magnifying lenses,
jeweler's goggles,
sometimes even the instruments of microsurgery.

Perhaps you have seen some of my pieces?
The Sun of Copernicus. The Ferris Wheel.
The Funeral Parlor (how difficult it was to glue the greenbottle fly
onto the right index finger of the corpse). Or
the one for which I am famous: *The Lovers of Late Afternoon.*
Her hair falling back, the red at the tip of his ear,
the universe of heated molecules, just above their bodies.

The Hours of Our Dreaming

e come, in sì poc' ora,
da sera a mane ha fatto il sol tragitto
—*Inferno*

I

I saw Dante in a hooded cape
exhaling a whir of cool breath over the bed
where my wife and I slept and turned

II

In an empty can of paint
a fly is trapped
and taps and ticks against the white gloom

III

The Queen Ant in the tunneled dark
will slowly eat her own wings like a martyr
Workers and slaves beware her little agonies

IV

Seven hundred years she has been dead
I walk out to see the stars
and through branches the slivered moon

V

A watermelon splits open in the warm night
Out of the pink flesh seeds rise up
fireflies

VI

If you want to have the dream of flying
I advise this   Hang your clothes upside down
Fill your shoes with air

VII

I'll tell nobody I saw Dante at sunrise
drinking bent from the rusty spigot
his cape and hood orange with fire

Inquiries

How did Tomás de Torquemada celebrate
his seventy-second birthday?

By taking a walk alone as the sun set
on the trees and the dry sticks underfoot?

By drinking a glass of red wine
after writing?

Or did he study in a mirror by candlelight
the growing lines of his nose and mouth?

———————

Was it in Aragón that the dark spider
fell by accident into his ear?

From what dream did he awake?

Or was it the brown scratching
that comes before dreaming?

———————

In what chair, by which window overlooking
the small river, did Torquemada read translations
of the Old Testament?

Did he love best the many rules of Leviticus?

———————

Was his favorite instrument
voice or stringed?

Which scared him more in the last years:
heat lightning, Ahura Mazdah,

or the rat chewing dry manuscripts in his death house?

The Yellow Borges: An Answer to a Question

Truth be told one whispered
I have bookends cast from Guevara's hands

Students of literature, omnivorous termites,
members of the fashionable brigade,
you have asked me to discuss the incident in question:
Yes, I remember the year I was fired at my incinerator job
because I could not destroy the silvertypes of my dead mother
I remember sitting unemployed on the fresh-cut grass
and the gold apple falling behind me
and there is a bird in the charcoal memory of that day
I knew by her wing beats: seven
The air was good, let's say, and I imagined plunging my hands
down into the thorax of John Milton (surely there was a flaw)

All of this happened exactly as I report it to you,
except for the apple, I confess
The basic fact is that twin lemons fell the morning
I lay in the lemon grass with my dead mother,
she reading Nietzsche to me as though he were Jesus:
"Can you compel the very stars to revolve around you?"
And, as I have told the Canadian woman whose breath is eucalyptus,
yes,
the detail of the bird is a fiction,
though there were probably some flies above us,
some distant ashes falling down,
a periphery of dandelion rays, of bells,
and this suggests another possibility:
it could be, you see, that I had achieved already the status of Minor Saint
and from broom closet to broom closet
midwived a village of confessions in the dark

Or, Brigadiers, if you come only for a simple truth:
the last thing I ever saw was the color yellow

Make-up

This is before Trotsky and Breton
before the murals of Diego Rivera
the intrusion of September 17
or the dream of wind and papaya

                    Green Coyoacán
in the bedroom mirror
Closing the left eyelid
Frida paints Orizaba
slowly
an ash triangle
rising up to the black brow
and a little moon
with a monkey's face
in the violet sky

Opening then on the dresser a Spanish fan
and fanning like a bird's wing till the coolness dries

                        She closes the other eye
                        and from memory makes up
                        a curving landscape of dark seeds
                        shiny inside the fruit
                        and the ghostly curl of one new life

            It is afternoon
Like a sleepwalker she moves to lie on the bed
Wind is blowing through an open window
This is before the little deer and the portraits
It involves the prophecy of being carried to the gallery
It is the revolution of one girl dreaming

The Story of Tapioca

For a year the man and the woman desired a child
and so swirled in the white sheets, hungry for gold.

The woman was a teacher; she read an anatomical manual.
She studied the calendar of her cycle like a yellow bible.

The man was born in the land of El Dorado. With wood
he worked by day. By moonlight he carved a straight wheat god.

With a compass the woman circled fertility windows
on their calendar. Be it Tuesday or the wind blow,

the woman and the man would bed until the oak beneath
them bend. Then they would sleep, quiet as breath.

The name of their future child they placed on their tongues
like chunks of papaya. They imagined a boy with black bangs.

On the fourth day of December when the woman
should have voided the 28 days, there was none,

only cold rain at daybreak, a spot, the small heat of fever.
The man whittled her a fan that opened to the scene of a river.

"By this time," she read, "the embryo is the size of a grain of wheat
or tapioca." Then there was a bright bleeding, and she grew hot.

On the fortieth day, she woke blurry in the surgical-blue gown.
In the stillness of recovery, she learned that part of her was gone.

How We Learn How Small Our Voice Is

The boy in the yard must be five,
the little visitor a girl not yet two, deaf.
She is pulling his orange toy mower.
The boy wears a bicycle helmet
and demands the attention of everything:
trees, grass, the stones in the driveway.
His mother is off to the side, trying to ignore him.
He tears a piece of bark from the oak and throws it.
He spits in the summer air.
He kicks the little lawn mower,
but she only walks away, in another direction.
Then he screams at her back with all his lung power
as he does to frighten the robins and the rabbits.
Nothing: she cannot hear him.
When finally he comes screaming into view, she smiles.
And still dragging the bright toy through the grass,
she waves with one hand to sign *Hello*.

Omens in a Small Town

> There's things going to happen in this town no one will talk about.
> —overheard at the Eat'n Park

Everyone you meet is either unemployed, a bow hunter,
or related by blood to one of the five undertakers.
To please the police, the bakery does dry cleaning.
The dogcatcher doubles as the priest. Often a long finger of clouds
blocks out the sun. Where the scrap yard ends, the college begins.
Yellow smoke rises from the brick stack on campus.
Something is poisoning the mourning doves.

You can feel the seal of the prothonotary
pressed in the green leaves of the Norway maples.
They keep your streets darker, the aphids fatter.
The borough council is suspected of arson.
An art professor nicknames you the Roman Martyr.
Your neighbors on either side seem overly fond
of the Middle Ages. Watercress grows wild
in the ditch of the Catholic cemetery. Perhaps worst of all:
the dentist tells you as he works he's hearing them again—
the voices of the arrows whizzing by in the dark.

Where Were You?

When the neck of our friend cracked
because of the weight of his body
in the black catch of the rope,
I was sitting down to a hot bowl
of wedding soup. It was peppery,
with escarole. The sun was shining.
A clock was ticking. And my wife was reaching up
to spray the top leaves of a spider plant.

The next day you, my brother, stood outside gazing
at your new cinder tiles and the downspout.
Your wife was backing out of the driveway,
her belly big as a moon in the white blouse.
When the phone rang, you were placing the mobile
above the crib, while long fingers were knotting
in another room the silk blossom of his yellow tie.

Ohiopyle Unrhymed

Ghosts in the white water never stay down.
A shirt balloons over rocks, exhales, comes back up.
I always wake a hundred miles from where I fell.

My body twists. My eyes spring to the green world:
rush of clouds, blue, swallow above the river.
Ghosts in the white water never stay down.

A body moving through foam could be a summer bird.
My head sinks. The search fails by helicopter, kayak.
I always wake a hundred miles from where I fell.

How bright the spirit leaves: orange, yellow, red,
like little fires on the river. My palms rise.
Ghosts in the white water never stay down.

Winter slows the river. Wind, iced branches,
snow falling in the dark. My eyes frozen in the morning sun,
I always wake a hundred miles from where I fell.

I hear enormous laughter just before the black.
Then feet dragging the riverbed. Moon. Flutter of moths.
I always wake a hundred miles from where I fell.
Ghosts in the white water never stay down.

The Other World

Un poema de poca sangre

Angel joven
mi nombre es José Asunción
y los senderos de mi país siempre he caminado
En las manos tengo un pájaro vivo y un cuchillo
En el espejo ovalado de la madrugada
ves claramente
el quetzal de plumas largas
de plumas verdes como hierba
la cabeza reclinada e inmóvil
el pico abierto hacia la primera luz de la mañana
y ya ves con claridad el cuchillo de plata
que me prestaba un ratero anónimo

Jovencito
si no quieres mirar
vuelve la cabeza
mientras corto suavemente
la garganta emplumada que tengo yo
Mi trabajo es robar
el canto verde y perfecto

A Poem of Little Blood

Young angel
my name is José Asunción
and I have walked the paths of my country endlessly
In my hands I hold a living bird and a knife
In the oval mirror of dawn
see clearly
the quetzal with long feathers
with feathers green like grass
the head reclined and still
the beak open toward the first light of morning
and now look carefully at the silver knife
lent to me by a nameless thief

Little One
if you don't want to watch
turn your head away
while I cut softly
the feathered throat
My work is to steal
the green and perfect song

To the Dead Farmer

It's no surprise to us.
We saw your death coming
in the parade of sugar ants on your bed sheet,
as the currucuy sang from the roof,
when the black butterfly entered your window,
when the steady hiss started in your ears
and you were late in pulling the blue onions.

Why did you refuse to pray against death?
Why did you deny us, our singing and our prayers?

The Straightest Branches

Still our imaginary house is made only of sticks,
only a frame nailed together of the straightest branches
my widowed father could find in the wild grove by the river
and shave down with machete to the bone-soft wood.
Last night the click and swish of his work
put me to sleep. He was already gone before sunrise
with wheelbarrow to look for scrap lumber, sheet metal,
plastic, and tarpaper. Always our chronic lack of nails.
When I awoke to the smell of his coffee,
I looked around quickly as I do now.
Un soplo de viento. A breath of wind
blew once through the ribs of this unfinished house.
How lonely the Andes are. Above me: stars, blue clouds,
the rustling air of eucalyptus. Prayers, chores. *Tinto* and some bread.
Then the birds becoming brighter on my long walk to school.

The Easter Revolt Painted on a Tablespoon

¿Dónde está el pueblo?
El pueblo ¿dónde está?
El pueblo está en las calles
buscando unidad.
Los pueblos unidos
jamás serán vencidos.
—popular chant

Above everything, I make a jagged, blue edge
and the Andes. Along the front and back of the handle,
I detail a greenhouse of fourteen thousand roses.
From the scooped tip as the tin rises, I place the president
of my country on the balcony of Hortua Hospital. Shouting
into an already antique microphone. Ordering the army
on horseback to charge. To destroy the squatters' camp.
I want you to hear the constant thudding, the long screams,
the galloping over mud. How it sounds
when the boy with five hundred roses
strapped to his back raises a burning branch
to touch the horse's chest. To show that motion: hooves
and the olive uniform falling through the mist. To freeze
the instant of boiling water splashed in the face
of a young corporal. I steady my hands to focus:
the quick slice of a bayonet through tarpaper, rocks in flight,
the revolvers popping until you can hear nothing buzz,
the hundred bodies of Policarpa filling up a common grave
in the pit of the tin spoon. I paint the basilica on fire,
as a wild, orange dove flies out of the stained glass.

On the back of the belled end, I make the other world:
where my mother lifts a clean shirt out of the aqueduct;
where my father shepherds our only cow, without a stick,
up the mountain from the grassy suburbs below.

The Tower in the Clouds

If
you
were
to
stack
all
of
the
tiny
white
coffins
of
my
country
from
the
ground
up
for
three
hundred
sixty-
five
thousand
days
and
nights
the
Andes
would
seem
like
the
stubble
of
new
grass
after
a
fire

At Twilight on the Road to Sogamoso

The sun is beginning to go down
over a field of yellow onions. The edges
of the clouds are almost pink, and at this hour
the maguey rises up like a flower of dark blades.
I worked so long today I have forgotten
my own hunger. It takes a full minute
for me to remember a word I have used
all my life. What the Mexicans call *poncho*.
At twilight I see it, abandoned, hanging like a ghost
on the limb of a tree: my own brown *ruana*
next to gray speckled chickens pecking at roots
and a black track of storm coming west over the green mountain.

The Archivist of Shadows

Los indios laches del norte de Boyacá adoraban sus propias sombras.
—Javier Ocampo López

Lights out!
Here is my life in a carousel of slides:
the insect pattern eaten from a leaf
the suicide mask of José Asunción
sweet ripe mango
the lion-tiger running across Laguna de Tota
a party of voices in a condemned house
the memory of my mother's fingertip on my neck
starlight
X-ray of a baby's hand
a cornfield in October
the painting of Our Lady of Chiquinquirá
the vibrations of this poem in Braille
quicksilver of papi's fingers over *cuatro* strings
the smell of wind through eucalyptus
lunar eclipse
ancient wings in rock
a hoofprint in snow
ashes
afterbirth buried in a hollow gourd
my gray hairs in a crow's nest
straw mat with corn drying
the dark second of a condor overhead
the letter O
sundial of an obelisk
the insect pattern eaten from a leaf

The thrill for me is after
on tongue and ear
the crunch of the green apple

In Nariño Nakopemda Balahika Sings, Dances, and Answers the Many Questions of Her Cinnamon Daughter

Mamita, who am I?
You are my Canela, my cinnamon one.

Mamita, who am I?
You are my beautiful daughter.

Mamita, who am I?
You are the reason for my Mali name.

Mamita, who am I?
You are the daughter of little storms.

Mamita, who is my father?
That man could be your father.
Or the one eating fried *yuca* in the shade.
Or the president giving a speech with his fist raised.
Or the one breathing fire for tourist coins.
Or that tree could be your father,
the fountain of green plumes and brown cocos.
Or the flying shadow of the blackbird could be him.
Even the pale skin stretched tight over the mouth of my drum.

Mamita, why did my father leave?
Perhaps he was ashamed of me.
Perhaps he was ashamed of his own pale skin.
Perhaps he loved his other wives more.

Mamita, when did he go?
He left on a white horse at the ghost hour.

Mamita, where did he go?
They say he went to a place called Koso
and swung from a rope knotted to a tree.
The people saw his head with a face on either side.

Mamita, why do you dance?
Because I am married to the wind.

Mamita, why do you dance?
Because I am married to the drum.

Mamita, what are the colors of your dancing?
They are the colors of the gourds:
orange and yellow and green and orange.

Mamita, what is the secret of your dancing?
Swing your dress like wings.
Tilt your shoulders like a bird.
Wear no shoes and stamp in the dirt.
Close your eyes. Listen to the rhythm of the river spirits.

Mamita, who gave you your spirit?
Abuelita, who taught me how to sing:
ooooo iiiiiiii   ooooo aaaaaaaa
ooo oioioioioioio aaa

Abuelita, who gave you your African name . . .
Nakopemda Balahika.
Here in Nariño it means
Yo Tengo Hambre de Tu Presencia.
I Am Hungry for Your Presence.
Now you know why when you were born
I named you my Canela. My sweet Canela.

I Sing on the Day of the Deceased

in memory of José Asunción Silva

> . . . sube a nacer conmigo, hermano.
> —Neftalí Reyes

I

Campesinos and green-tailed birds eat gladly from the strawberries
and morning glories twisting
up the trellis of my spine
I play turtleback guitar   ghost flute   conch
I am nothing but bone and American song

II

I am zero

I am dogwood flowering pink

I am the little howls of Chiapas

I am the moan in the *caracol* at Guayaquil

I sing against the National Police who violated her small body

I cup my hands over my skull to hear stars

I am the catch in the throat of Quechua

I am the baby shepherd in a pen of *cuy*

I am the voice of corn and *yuca*

I am drums I am Changó *el gran putas*

I root into the wall of you

I am the wizened Aleut praying in the Russian Church

I know the world is wide and alien and emerald

I ride with Edchewe on the perilous journey to sun and moon

III

I am your brother   lover   sister   *bisabuelo*

these bones

Eat from my vines the rubies   the funnels of blue

Listen to the sound of rain on stone

The flute I blow

was once that happy arm that held you in the dark

Homage to My Emerald Body

to Aurelio Arturo

On this green leaf I sketched for you
the long curves of my thighs
the moss like delicate silk
growing endlessly in my throat
my mint eyes   morning stars
the meadow of lost crickets
dreaming in my ear

In that twilight
when the distant sky
appeared even more blue than pink
we heard for the first time
the heart's echo like a pistol
and from a thermos you poured me
a demitasse of *tinto* with steam
a bowl of pure air
and finally you shared with me
in the middle of Boyacense woods
the bread of your body
naked and open and hungry

On this leaf
already the color of wheat at harvest
I want you to hear me forever
in the cooing of the invisible doves
in the murmur of the river Chicamocha
in the silence of large white clouds

Some day some morning
I'll wake in your bed filled with sunlight
my hair long and my bones made of emeralds

Homenaje a mi cuerpo de esmeralda

a Aurelio Arturo

En esta hoja verde te dibujé
las curvas largas de los muslos míos
el musgo como seda delicada
que crece sin fin en la garganta
mis ojos de menta   mis luceros de la mañana
la pradera de grillos perdidos
soñando en el oído

En aquel crepúsculo
cuando los cielos en la distancia
parecían aún más azules que rosados
oímos por primera vez el eco
de la pistola del corazón y de un termo
me diste una tacita de tinto con vapor
un tazón de puro aire
y por fin me compartiste
en el medio del bosque boyacense
el pan del cuerpo tuyo
desnudo y abierto y hambriento

En esta hoja ya el color de espigas
en el momento de la cosecha
quiero que me oigas para siempre
en el arrullo de las palomas invisibles
en el murmullo del río Chicamocha
en el silencio de las nubes enormes y blancas

Algún día por la mañana
me despertaré en tu lecho lleno de sol
con cabellos largos y huesos de esmeralda

Acknowledgments

I gratefully acknowledge the following publications in which these poems first appeared: *The Bloomsbury Review* ("Make-up"); *The Kenyon Review* (section I in "The River Spirits" as "Spirit" and "To the Dead Farmer"); *Parnassus: Poetry in Review* ("Doña Josefina Counsels Doña Concepción Before Entering Sears," "How Grammar School Is Changing"); *The Pennsylvania Review* ("The Yellow Borges: An Answer to a Question"); *The Pittsburgh Post-Gazette* (section VIII in "The River Spirits" as "Hazelwood").

I would also like to thank Janet Jennerjohn for continuing to edit, improve, and shape my work.

Y muchísimas gracias a Diego Eduardo por darnos luz y alegría.

Maurice Kilwein Guevara was born in Belencito, Colombia in 1961 and raised in Pittsburgh, Pennsylvania. He was educated at the University of Pittsburgh, Bowling Green State University, and the University of Wisconsin, Milwaukee. He has received awards from the Bread Loaf Writers' Conference, the J. William Fulbright Commission, the Pennsylvania Council on the Arts, and the Pennsylvania Humanities Council. His first book of poetry, *Postmortem,* was published in 1994. Kilwein Guevara has given poetry readings in Colombia, Mexico, and throughout the United States. His work has appeared in *Poetry, Kenyon Review, Bloomsbury Review, Exquisite Corpse,* and other literary magazines. He teaches literature and writing at Indiana University of Pennsylvania. He is married to Janet Jennerjohn, and they have a son, Diego Eduardo.

Library of Congress Cataloging-in-Publication Data

Kilwein Guevara, Maurice
    Poems of the river spirit / by Maurice Kilwein Guevara.
        p.   cm.
    ISBN 0-8229-3934-7 (cloth : alk. paper). — ISBN 0-8229-5591-1
(paper : alk. paper)
    I. Title.
PS3561.I4135P64   1996
811'.54—dc20   95-43298